Penny Stocks

Everything You Should Know To Get Started And Earn Big + Common Mistakes Made By Newbies And How To Avoid Them

Jacob Grant

© **Copyright 2017 by Jacob Grant - All rights reserved.**

The follow eBook is reproduced below with the goal of providing information that is as accurate and reliable as possible. Regardless, purchasing this eBook can be seen as consent to the fact that both the publisher and the author of this book are in no way experts on the topics discussed within and that any recommendations or suggestions that are made herein are for entertainment purposes only. Professionals should be consulted as needed prior to undertaking any of the action endorsed herein.

This declaration is deemed fair and valid by both the American Bar Association and the Committee of Publishers Association and is legally binding throughout the United States.

Furthermore, the transmission, duplication or reproduction of any of the following work including specific information will be considered an illegal act irrespective of if it is done electronically or in print. This extends to creating a secondary or tertiary copy of the work or a recorded copy and is only allowed with express written consent from the Publisher. All additional right reserved.

The information in the following pages is broadly considered to be a truthful and accurate account of facts and as such any inattention, use or misuse of the information in question by the reader will render any resulting actions solely under their purview. There are no scenarios in which the publisher or the original author of this work can be in any fashion deemed liable for any hardship or damages that may befall them after undertaking information described herein.

Additionally, the information in the following pages is intended only for informational purposes and should thus be thought of as universal. As befitting its nature, it is presented without assurance regarding its prolonged validity or interim quality. Trademarks that are mentioned are done without written consent and can in no way be considered an endorsement from the trademark holder.

TABLE OF CONTENTS

Introduction 1
Chapter 1: Understanding Penny Stocks 2
Chapter 2: The Risks and Benefits of Investing in Penny Stocks............ 8
Chapter 3: The Keys to Success... 13
Chapter 4: Start Trading 21
Chapter 5: Common Pitfalls and How to Avoid Them 34
Conclusion 40
Description 41

Introduction

Congratulations on downloading this book and thank you for doing so.

The following chapters will discuss everything you need to know about penny stocks. They will explain to you what penny stocks are, how to make money by investing in and trading penny stocks, as well as the common pitfalls that you should avoid, and more!

There are plenty of books on this subject on the market, thanks again for choosing this one! Every effort was made to ensure it is full of as much useful information as possible, please enjoy!

Chapter 1: Understanding Penny Stocks

As the name already implies, penny stocks are stocks that have a low price per share. They are also called *cent stocks* or *penny shares*. However, they do not literally worth a penny or a cent.

In the past, any stock worth less than a dollar per share was considered a penny stock. However, the U.S. SEC modified the definition of a penny stock. Now, any stock with a price of less than $5 per share is considered a penny stock. In the U.K., any stock with a price of less than £1 falls under the category of a penny stock.

Due to their relatively low value, most penny stocks cannot be found in the major market exchanges, and are only traded by small companies. But, there are still a few huge and well-established companies that trade penny stocks on major exchanges.

Is investing in penny stocks for you?

Investing in penny stocks is like playing slots or video poker in a casino. Penny stocks have a high volatility. This means that their value fluctuates dramatically, where significant changes in their price usually occur. A penny stock priced at $4 can drop down to 50% or lower within a short period of time. However, the high volatility of penny stocks is also one of the main reasons why many people love to invest in them. A penny stock today may no longer be a penny stock tomorrow. Just as a penny stock's price can decrease dramatically within a short period of time, it can also increase significantly.

Therefore, if you do not want to take so much risk, or if you would rather have small but almost guaranteed gains or income, then it would be better for you not to consider investing in penny stocks. You would do much better investing in blue-chip stocks. However, if you have some money to spend, and you do not mind investing in something that has a high volatility with a low probability (but still possible) of making high returns on your investment, then investing in penny stocks would be an excellent choice.

Another option which may be considered more practical is for you to invest a big part of your funds in something that is less risky and, at the same time, invest a small part of your funds in penny stocks. This way you will be more open to opportunities without having to worry so much about losing all your investment.

Investing vs. trading

This book uses both terms synonymously. There is almost no difference between investing in and trading penny stocks. However, for the word geeks out there, investing is simply buying penny stocks hoping that their value will increase after some time. The investor can then sell it at a higher price if he chooses to do so, or he can just keep them for a longer period. Trading is more active. The value of penny stocks fluctuates even in a 24-hour time. Therefore, you can expect to make multiple trades in a week. The prices of penny stocks can be seen increasing and decreasing almost randomly. The goal of every penny stocks trader follows the famous principle: Buy when the price is low, and sell when the price is high. However, when dealing with penny stocks, said principle is not absolute. You cannot just buy anything that has a low price and proper timing is essential when selling.

Penny stocks vs. blue-chip stocks

Although both are stocks issued by companies, there are certain differences between the two.

Volatility

Penny stocks are highly volatile. Such high volatility is what will make you earn more money or lose your money quickly. Blue-chip stocks are more secure with low volatility.

Speculative

On the one hand, penny stocks are highly speculative; therefore, investing in penny stocks is riskier. On the other hand, investing in blue-chip stocks has less risk due because they have little speculative value.

Dividends

You can barely receive any dividends from penny stocks, while blue-chip stocks usually pay dividends.

Sensitivity

Penny stocks are more sensitive to various sector influences, which easily affect the price of the stocks to rise or fall. Blue-chip stocks are less affected by such influences. This is another reason why blue-chip stocks are more secure.

Profit potential

Investing in penny stocks has a higher profit potential; however, the risk is also higher. Of course, blue-chip stocks have a more secure profit potential. However, to earn a decent amount of profit, you will have to invest more money because blue-chip stocks usually have a low-profit margin.

Availability of data

Penny stocks are less transparent than blue-chip stocks. Therefore, you will have less data to analyze. The information that you can get from research is also limited. This makes it more difficult to know if you are really making a good investment decision because there will be many unknown factors to deal with. Blue-chip stocks are well known. Many popular companies have an open book of information regarding the company, so it will be easier to tell if the business is doing good or not.

Penny stock volatility

Penny stocks are known for having high volatility. They usually take dramatic price swings, which make investors to either lose their money or make a good amount of income.

First, let us discuss what *volatility* is. Volatility simply means rapid and unpredictable changes. Therefore, when we say high volatility in stocks, it means that the price of a certain stock changes quickly and significantly. Meaning, such significant price swings are sure to happen. The prices of certain stocks will rise and fall almost randomly.

Here are the common causes that affect the volatility of penny stocks:

Investors themselves

There are many factors that affect the volatility of the penny stock market. The activity of many investors of buying and selling affects volatility. Investors have different preferences as to when to buy or sell stocks, as well as which ones to buy or sell. Of course, this is something outside of your control.

Government laws and policies

The government has an active interest in businesses and the market. This is also for the protection of the people. The enactment of laws and government policies what affect businesses also contribute to the volatility of the penny stock market, because said laws and policies influence businesses, investors, and even market behavior.

Economic problems

The economy is one of the key factors that strongly affect the prices of stocks in the market. Economic problems, if left unresolved and become serious, can create a domino effect that will pull down not only the prices of stocks but also the ordinary people. This will influence many other investments, consumer confidence, even the pension payouts.

Reports

Publicly-traded companies file their financial reports on a regular basis. Although not a good basis for making a decision as to which stocks to buy or sell, once these reports from various companies are made public, they affect the behavior of many investors.

Volatile nature

It is the nature of the market to be volatile. Because the market is not just about stock certificates, packaging, goods, and services—the market is alive. It is run by people who have their own ideas, interests, and preferences. The prices of stocks continue to move just as many businesses do.

Consumer behavior

How the market responds to businesses is another major

factor that affects the volatility of stocks. Just as businesses grow, the prices of their stocks also increase. However, consumers are not robots. A person may like a product today but would prefer to buy a different product or brand tomorrow.

Competition

Although competition among businesses benefits consumers by virtue of the fact that they're assured of good and quality products and services, said competition also causes the volatility of stocks. As one business enterprise dominates another, the value of its stocks will increase, but the prices of stocks of the other enterprise will decrease.

These, among many others, affect the volatility of stocks. This is also the reason why it is hard to compute whether the prices of certain stocks will rise or fall within a specified period: simply because there are so many factors to consider. And, most of these factors are outside your control. Even many skilled investors are known for losing money by investing in stocks, including penny stocks. But, do not let this discourage you. Still, there are those who are very happy with their investment in penny stocks.

Take advantage of price swings

The uncontrollable price swings are the key to profit. You should buy penny stocks at a low price then sell them when their price goes up. As they say, patience is a virtue. It is the same when investing in penny stocks. Many times you will have to wait for the value of your stocks to increase. Since high volatility is in the nature of penny stocks, you can expect the prices to shoot up; however, if unlucky, you can also encounter a significant decrease in value.

Chapter 2: The Risks and Benefits of Investing in Penny Stocks

There are two things investing in penny stocks are very much known for:

1. Potential of making a big income
2. A high probability of losing your investment

The goal, of course, is to turn that potential of making a big income into a reality. However, the unfortunate truth is that like the game of slots in the casino, most people who invest in penny stocks lose their money, and only a few end up happy with their investment.

In order lower your chances of losing your investment, you should understand the risks that are associated with investing in penny stocks.

The risks

Bankruptcy

Most companies that deal with penny stocks are either small companies or those that are about to go bankrupt. Of course, these companies that are about to declare bankruptcy will not disclose to you that the company is already falling into pieces. Now, when you invest in its penny stocks, you will be considered as a mere common stockholder — and you will have no control over what the company does with its assets. In the event that the company finally declares and there is no way it can pay out its debts to its creditors (and this is normal), its assets will be sold and you will not receive anything. Nothing. It is a 0$ game where you lose everything.

Start-up companies

Most companies that issue penny stocks are usually new and small. Therefore, there is no way you can track their history. You would not be certain whether you are dealing with a legitimate company or simply one of the scammers out there who will rip you off of your money. And, since penny stocks are usually traded by small companies, and small companies do not get so much attention, mismanagement becomes an issue where the executives of the company see the assets of the business as their own property without regard to the claim of ownership of the other stockholders, including penny stockholders.

Less transparent

Considering their low value, penny stocks have less stringent requirements. In fact, they are mostly traded on the pink sheets or simply over the counter (OTC). Companies on the pink sheets do not file with the SEC nor are they required to meet certain requirements as to the minimum capitalization or capital stock. Therefore, you cannot get accurate information about such companies. These companies are on the pink sheet either because they are so small and cannot meet the minimum requirement or simply want to hide their information from the public. The Pink Sheets is privately owned and is also considered an over-the-counter market without any centralized trading floor. OTC simply means that the stocks are traded in a manner other than the centralized, strongly regulated, and formal exchange such as the New York Stock Exchange.

Low liquidity

The way to make money with penny stocks is to sell them once their price increases. However, since penny stocks have low liquidity, it is difficult to get a buyer. Its low liquidity level also makes it prone to manipulation where its value gets hyped up to make them look attractive then sell them to investors. This is also known as the *pump and dump*. As the name implies, first the value of a stock is pumped up with some marketing or promotional hype then when an investor buys it thinking that it is an attractive investment, it gets *dumped* on the investor. What happens here is the price suddenly falls down and the investor will be at a loss.

It is worth nothing that this fraudulent scheme can also be used even when the company is doing well. In fact, it becomes more convincing to pump and dump the prices of stocks when their price is actually increasing. By adding a dollar or two on top of its actual price while it is increasing, it becomes difficult for investors to find out if the said price is being pumped or is really the effect of the growing stock value of the company.

Speculative

Investing in penny stocks can be said to be speculative. There are simply a number of factors that must meet and work to your advantage in order to make a profit. First, you must be able to buy a stock that really has a potential to make a profit. With many people who are good at overselling the qualities of a penny stock, it is difficult to identify which ones really have a good value for its price. Second, even if you have bought a good stock at a low cost, there are many factors that can affect its performance. Therefore, there is no guaranteed assurance that its price will increase. And, even if you get lucky and the price of your stock increases, there is no assurance that it will continue to turn into a significant amount. Last but not least, considering the low liquidity of penny stocks, who would be your buyer? Will the market still consider your stocks profitable by the time you offer them for sale? If yes, then why sell them?

These, among other things, are the risks faced by many people who invest in penny stocks. Is this still a good investment? It is true that most suffer continuous losses, but there are still those who make a decent amount of profit. After all, you can invest in penny stocks even with a low capital. This makes them exciting and also lucrative. Despite the clear disadvantage and factual records that investors lose in this kind of investment, there is still a chance to make a huge amount of money out of it.

The Benefits

Investing in penny stocks is truly challenging. But, if you think you are up for the challenge, if such high risk and volatility do not crush your entrepreneurial spirit, then welcome to the world of penny stocks—a world of high profits where stakes are low but the rewards are high; the business where you can invest a little and earn a lot; where you can double, triple, or even multiply your every investment more than five times.

Price

A single penny stock only costs less than $5, so you can invest in penny stocks with just a small capital. If you are an investor on a budget, then this is the one for you.

High potential return

Most companies that offer penny stocks are the small ones—the ones that are developing and have a lot of space for improvements. As they improve, the value of their stocks also increases, including the price of their penny stocks. Therefore, it is possible to earn more by investing a little in penny stocks than investing a huge amount in high-priced stocks of well-established companies that will only give you a small increase in value after a period of time. It is not surprising for penny stocks to double their value in a single trading day.

Low or controlled loss

Unless you invest millions in penny stocks, then your expected loss will be minimized since penny stocks are cheap. Moreover, out of the different penny stocks that you invest in, a few of them can give you a good return, which can minimize your overall losses, if any.

High volume

Since penny stocks are very affordable, you can easily purchase lots of stocks even if you only had $5,000 (or even less). This high volume is also good, especially when you purchase stocks from a start-up company that grows well. This will allow you to soon hold many stocks with a high value. Having a high volume for a low price will also enable you to diversify your stocks at a low cost.

Chapter 3: The Keys to Success

Like a video poker game, success in investing in penny stocks does not come from pure luck. There are elements that you can use to increase your chances of making a profit. Like any other venture that is worth pursuing, this takes hard work, patience, skill, and practice.

Do your research

Do not just research about the stocks that you plan to buy. You can have a better understanding and thereby increase your chances of success by doing a more comprehensive research: Research the business itself. Find out when the business started, its performance in the market, and how it matches up with its competitors. The more you know about the company from which you will get your stocks, the higher is the probability of choosing the right penny stocks to invest in.

Observe the trends

Study the graphs and tables that display how a certain stock performs. Do not just limit yourself to its weekly record. If possible, check how its price rises and falls for several weeks, even months—or even a year. And do not limit yourself to just one company no matter how popular it may be. Study other companies and the penny stocks that they offer.

Many investors rely heavily on the latest trends when making an investment decision. Although you cannot ignore the latest trends, take note that such trends only show the current performance of the company and that there are many other factors that will affect its performance in the near future. Moreover, trends change—and most of the time, they change quickly.

Know the latest news

Read the newspapers and be aware of the latest news. There are many factors that affect the prices of penny stocks, such as laws, new businesses, new trends, among other things. By analyzing the news, you will have additional information to foresee which stocks will perform well in the near future. However, it is worth noting that merely analyzing how the news can impact the stock market is not sufficient. Still, what matters is the actual prices of the penny stocks, and how they move in the marketplace.

Only invest the money you can afford to lose

"Only play with the money you can afford to lose." This is a common advice given to gamblers. Like gambling, there is no guarantee that investing in penny stocks will make any profit. There is always the possibility that you can lose your investment. Therefore, do not use the money that you have for your electric bill or other obligations that you need to pay.

Set a limit

Penny stocks have high volatility. On the one hand, if you continue to hold on to a stock whose price has been continuously increasing, it will soon reach its peak and begin decreasing. On the other hand, if you continue to keep losing stocks, decide up to what point you will continue to hold on to them. At which point, you will have to sell them. Although this will not yield any profit, it can help to minimize your losses.

Look for patterns

The movement of penny stocks can be said to be random. Due to the great many factors that influence their prices, their values rise and fall almost unpredictably. However, even randomness creates certain patterns within a period of time.

If you can spot these patterns, you will have higher chances of identifying and buying the right penny stocks.

Make your own decision

Do not just buy the stocks that "experts" promote online. Develop your own understanding of how penny stocks work in the market, and make your own decision. For example, if you see someone promoting stock X as a profitable investment, ask yourself why it is profitable, and what makes it different from all the other stocks. Is it truly a profitable investment? Mind you, there are many people who promote stocks only to serve their own interest, purely for their own personal gain. So, be careful, and always take everything you hear or read with a grain of salt.

Do not chase after your losses

Never chase after your losses. If you do, there is a big probability that you will only lose more. Accept your losses when they happen. In fact, expect to encounter a number of losing trades/investments. Penny stocks are very volatile; it is normal to see their value decreasing.

Stay calm

Even when you encounter some losing streaks or a series of "wrong" investments, you must stay calm and keep your cool. When you trade penny stocks long enough, you will realize that bad days do occur, and it is normal.

Do not be greedy

The 50% you gained yesterday may start decreasing today. Learn not to be greedy. Make a decision to see, take your profit, and cash out.

Keep your emotion under control

Although it is good to have passion in what you do, when you invest in penny stocks, never allow your emotion to take control of your decision. Keep your emotion in check and never buy or sell stocks when under pressure. Remember that investing in or trading penny stocks is a business. You have to be smart and not allow your emotion to cloud your judgment.

Stick to the plan

Some investors come up with a plan, execute it, only to change the plan abruptly once they encounter a sudden decrease in the price of their chosen stocks. This is a common mistake. Remember to stick to your original plan; otherwise, you will not know if such chosen strategy works or not. In making a plan, consider the volatility of penny stocks. Of course, there are instances where you need to let go of your original plan, such as when a big loss is imminent. However, when you change your original plan, make sure that you have a better and well-planned strategy to take its place.

Only invest in penny stocks that have a high volume

Illiquidity is one of the major problems of investing in penny stocks. Even if the value of your stocks increases, how can you make real profit if no one wants to buy them? Therefore, only invest in penny stocks that get a good amount of trades per day. According to some "expert," only invest in stocks that trade at least a hundred thousand shares per day.

Pump your stocks

Buy cheap penny stock, market them as something valuable, then sell them at a premium price, or at least at a price where you can get a decent profit. Yes, this is how the pump and dump scheme works—and if you do not mind, you can do it, too. Write and send out newsletters. You can even put up a blog and be an "expert" in the field of trading penny stocks, then sell the stocks that you have with your persuasive marketing skills.

Get the latest updates quickly

The trend of penny stocks is simple: the prices rise and fall. This trend happens whether the cause of the increase or decrease is due to legitimate means or not. High volatility is simply in the nature of penny stocks. Therefore, there are two things to remember:

1. Be sure to get the latest updates on penny stocks as soon as they are out. Or, if you can, know them before they get released in public; and
2. Make sure that those stocks are being promoted.

So, how do you make money off of this? Simple. Identify some good penny stocks and buy them just before their price increase or at the initial stage of its price increase. Now, since other people will promote the stocks, you can take advantage of their hard labor for free and watch your stocks' price increase. Aim for a low profit of just 5%-10%, and then sell them right away. This is an easy way to earn money almost regularly. However, if you want more adventure, then you can continue to hold on to your stocks for as long as you want, which is a lot riskier.

Focus on start-up companies

This is an excellent way of finding the best penny stocks to invest in. However, this also takes some serious work. But, if you want to take investing in penny stocks more seriously, then this would be truly helpful.

Research and study the different start-up companies that offer penny stocks. Spot the best company in terms of performance against its competitors, as well as the amount of profit that it makes. A growing company has so much room for development, and as it grows, the price of its stocks also increases. If you manage to spot a good and legitimate start-up company, buy some penny stocks and let the company work for you.

You do not have to sell the stocks right away, especially if the company demonstrates continuous development. If you want, you can simply sell even up to 50% of your stocks, but it is not advised that you withdraw all your stocks at once at this point.

The lazy method

This method is not recommended, but you might want to do it for fun, especially when you are too lazy to make any research.

Simply invest in particular penny stocks that are gaining popularity, hope for some luck as you wait for the price to increase, then sell. You can easily find out which ones are drawing interest by joining different forums on penny stocks and related websites.

Keep a journal

Write down every move or trade that you make. This will allow you to think outside the box and be more rational when making decisions. This can also help to make you realize some weaknesses or wrong investment decisions. If you think writing is such a big task, you can just type your experiences using any writing software or application. Update your journal regularly. Make sure it reflects every trade that you do, so you can have a better view of your whole investment.

Take a break

Investing in penny stocks can be addicting. You may get into the habit of checking the prices now and then and looking for any effective strategy online from some "experts." But, do not forget about yourself and your family. Learn to step back for a moment and take a break. You can think more clearly if you give yourself enough rest.

Have fun

Whether you make a profit or not, it is always good to have fun. Investing in penny stocks, after all, is really fun. It is like gambling. Hence, it is also addicting. Have fun; enjoy every profit and take it easy when you encounter a loss.

Choosing the right penny stocks

There is no absolute rule that can guarantee that the value of certain penny stocks will increase. If such were the case, investors would always make money by investing in penny stocks. However, there are factors that you need to understand which can increase your chances of making a profit.

Profit can come in many ways: The price of a low-priced stock can increase; the price of a stock whose price has already increased can continue to increase; or the price of a stock whose price has just decreased can soon increase. Regardless of which way happens for you, you need someone to buy your stocks to make a real profit.

Be patient

Although you can trade penny stocks within 24 hours, it is best to have a strategy that will last for a few days. Be patient and wait for the high volatility of penny stocks to work to your advantage. However, do not wait too long; otherwise, the trend might start to work against you.

Use the high volatility to your advantage

The high volatility of penny stocks is often what discourages people from investing. However, just as every cause has an equal and opposite reaction, you can use the fluctuating value of penny stocks to your advantage.

If you combine all the different information that we have already discussed, you will have different factors that greatly affect the dramatic price swings of penny stocks. Study these factors and make said high volatility to work in your favor.

Chapter 4: Start Trading

The best way to learn how to invest and trade penny stocks is through actual practice. So, if you are ready to take the challenge and start earning money, it is time to get to the actual application.

Create an account

To invest in and trade penny stocks, you need to make an account with a trustworthy platform where you can buy and sell penny stocks. This is called an investment trading account. Do not worry; registration is usually fast and simple.

Online platforms differ from one another. Be sure to use the one that suits your needs. Some trading platforms require a minimum deposit, while others do not.

Once you have access to your account and deposited some funds, you can now buy your first penny stocks with a click of a mouse and start trading.

The following are popular platforms used by many investors and traders of penny stocks:

- Charles Schwab (www.schwab.com)
- TradeKing (www.tradeking.com)
- E*Trade (us.etrade.com)
- TD Ameritrade (www.tdameritrade.com)
- Interactive Brokers (www.interactivebrokers.com.hk)
- OptionsHouse (www.optionshouse.com)
- Scottrade (www.scottrade.com)

This list is not exclusive, so keep your eye out for other trustworthy platforms that would best serve your interests.

Practice game

After registration, most trading platforms will allow you to have a real-time simulation by giving you free virtual credits. You cannot withdraw said credit balance and any profit that you get from it is not convertible into cash. Treat it as a warm up, practice game. And yes, this is highly recommended. Even if you think you already understand how penny stocks work, even if you firmly believe in your strategy, you should invest some time and effort in some practice. This can help cut down some losses.

Start small

Whether or not you make use of the virtual credits, or even if you have a high capital to invest, it is good to start small. Even by starting out small, you will still experience actual gains (or losses). Especially for beginners, beginning with a small investment will help you boost your confidence. After all, if you truly have a good strategy, you can easily increase your investment to earn more profit.

The strategies

There are a number of strategies to choose from when investing in penny stocks. However, you can only use one strategy at a time. Some follow certain popular strategies faithfully, but it is advised that you simply learn from the already existing strategies and try to develop your own. After all, despite the so many strategies out there which tell you how to make money with penny stocks, the significant majority of investors still lose their money or earn very little from their investment.

Focus on the company

It is important that you focus on the company, more specifically, on its quarterly earnings and sales. Again, always do your research. No matter how big the media coverage is or the extent of marketing involved, penny stocks will only increase their value if the company earns a good amount of income.

Avoid pink sheet penny stocks

Although it is tempting to purchase your first stocks from pink sheet because of the attractive, low prices that are offered, it is still a risky move. Pink sheet stocks do not need to meet certain requirements and are not even regulated by the SEC. Most of the pink sheet companies are either so small that they are struggling to stay in business or are just about to go bankrupt. Worse, some of them will just scam you.

Limit your orders

The high volatility of penny stocks can create a drastic increase and decrease in price within one trading day. When buying penny stocks, you can set a limit for your order. For example, you can set a buy price of maybe 15 cents higher than the previous day's amount—then you can apply a limit order to avoid overpayment. The same applies when selling: you can cap a limit to what you think is the best selling price, if you hit the mark, then good, but if not, then just try again tomorrow. At least, you still get to keep your stocks and lose nothing.

Limit orders do the job for you. You do not have to keep watch on the computer all the time just to monitor the prices so you can buy or sell a penny stock. When trading penny stocks, there are two essential keys to master: Choosing the best penny stocks to invest in, and how you use limit orders (for buying and selling).

Stop-loss limit

Stop loss is a way to prevent you from chasing after your losses, so you will not lose more money. Many who do little work just continue to hold on to their penny stocks despite a massive decrease in value hoping that the price will soon pick up on the reasoning that volatility is in the nature of penny stocks. Although this seems true in some respect, it is also one of the reasons why many investments fail. Unlike blue chips, penny stocks are highly volatile. So, set a stop-loss limit. For example, if you set a limit of 30%, if the price of your penny stocks goes down and reaches 30%, sell the stocks, accept your losses, and start over. Another variation is simply to sell 50% of your investment in the said stocks and let the other 50% ride the flow and hope for the best.

Keep your profit

Another strategy is to always keep your profit, so you can cut down losses and hopefully earn more. For example, once you make a profit, sell a number of stocks that is equivalent to your earned profit. So, you will be left with your original investment still active in play, plus some profit that is already in a safe place (unless you invest said profit again).

Save your investment

A similar strategy is to sell your stocks equivalent to your original investment after a significant increase in value and simply continue investing with the profit that you have already earned. This way, you will not lose anything even if your new investment (second investment taken from the profits of the original investment) fails to make any profit.

Lighten your position

If certain penny stocks get a significant increase in value, but there is no news about it, chances are their price will soon drop. So, lighten your position by selling them before they drop. You can also just sell a few and have the other stocks to ride the flow.

Focus on the numbers

Ignore the "noise" and focus on the numbers. The truthfulness of what people, online marketers, so-called "experts", and what the media say is hard to know. However, numbers do not lie. If you look close enough, they can reveal to you which stocks have the highest potential of making a profit and those that you should stay away from.

Reassess your strategy

Reassess your strategy from time to time, especially when there is a change in circumstances. The volatility of penny stocks depends on many factors, and a single factor has the potential to make drastic changes. Check your strategy from time to time, and be sure that it matches up well with the changes in the stock market.

Learn from your mistakes

Committing mistakes is a part of the learning process. Do not be too emotional when you lose a trade. Instead, study the situation and the attending circumstances. Find out what made you decide that way, and how come the result was not as expected. Be logical and rational about it. Always look for explanations and learn. Mistakes are not always a bad loss. Sometimes, they are just the price that you have to pay for learning something valuable. So, be prepared to commit mistakes. Learn and move on.

Develop your strategy

Just as the penny stock market is a continuously moving and growing market, your strategy should also be flexible enough to adapt to changes and continuously develop.

Buy/Sell order

The procedure to make a buy order depends on the platform that you use. Basically, there are 8 steps:

1. Select or click the Buy button.
2. Type the number of shares that you want to purchase.
3. Use the All or None option.
4. Select the appropriate stock symbol.
5. Select limit order (to avoid overpaying).
6. Under duration, choose Today.
7. Key in the asking price.
8. Select complete, finish, or submit.

Here are the basic procedures for making a sell order:

1. Select sell.
2. Enter the number of shares that you want to sell.
3. Enter or select the appropriate stock symbol.
4. Use the All or None option.
5. You may select the limit order to avoid overselling.
6. Choose today as duration.
7. Key in the bid price.
8. Select finish, complete, or submit.

Online platforms always have a tutorial or guidelines, as well as customer service to assist you. Do not hesitate to ask for their help. Fortunately, most of the popular trading platforms online use a fairly intuitive system that is very easy to understand. Be sure to check the FAQ section, the given guidelines or tutorial, make use of the free virtual credits, and contact Support for any assistance or clarifications that you need.

When to buy

The best time to buy a penny stock is not only when the price is low, but also when there is an expected increase in its price. Also, it is not only about when you should buy but also which penny stocks to purchase. Being able to identify the best penny stocks to invest in takes a good amount of research, time, and practice.

When to sell

Selling your stocks is the process where you convert the stocks into cash. This is where you experience the real income of your investment. But, when do you sell? It is advised that before you even begin buying or trading a particular stock, you must already have a target percentage of profit. Say, for example, 20%. Now, once the price of the said stock reaches your target percentage (in this case, 20%), sell it immediately. Most people who invest in penny stocks do not just lose money for failing to choose the right stocks, many lose their invested money because they hold on to a stock for too long until they are beaten by the high volatility that is inherent in the penny stock market.

Discipline and self-control are important. Once you hit your target percentage of profit, sell your stocks and start over. This is the general rule. An exception is when the trend is so clear and strong that it would be irrational to sell your stocks right away. For example, when the said stocks are all over the news and have clearly captured the market's interest.

Stock split

A stock split is where the company enacts to split its stocks.

Therefore, if you have one share, it will become two shares. This is applicable to every share that you have. So, if you have 200,000 shares, you will have 400,000 shares. The price also gets split. If each share costs $2, then the price will become $1. Simple and fair enough. A stock split is actually a good sign. It means that the company is growing. A stock split is often made by a company whose shares have already gained some significant increase in value.

Reverse split

This is something you have to watch out for, because it is not good for you. Companies usually resort to this as an attempt to save its business from bankruptcy. It is a clear sign that something is wrong with the company, and that it is struggling to survive. Example: Let us say there is 1 for every 20 reverse splits. The effect is that every 20 shares you have will be counted as a single share, but its price will be equivalent to 20 shares. Therefore, when you or another investor looks at it, it is like Company X's stocks have grown by leaps and bounds when, in fact, the price was only manipulated to appear like an attractive investment.

"Buy the rumor, sell the fact."

This is a common saying that should be understood and applied by every trader. Novice traders would do so much better if they understand what this means. So, what is this saying?

When a big event or business move is about to happen, rumors spread quickly, which draw a lot of interest in the stocks concerned. Investors make a buy in, convinced that the price of the stocks will leap. The problem is, once the event takes place, it does not make such surge in price anymore, because of the price increase that already happened prior to the date of the actual event. Now, this is where the price of the stocks begins to dwindle down and where loss of investment becomes imminent.

But, as you can see, there is a lesson here. In fact, this gives rise to a golden opportunity. By buying the rumor (meaning, buying the stocks during the rumor), the value of the stocks that you buy will increase dramatically. The next move is simply to sell the fact. This means that you should sell the stocks before their price begins to dwindle down. Many investors make the common mistake of being too greedy and continue to hold on to their stocks for too long. Remember, once the price hits the ceiling and the prices begin to fall down, it will be very hard to sell those stocks for a profit.

So, what should you do? Answer: Buy the stocks as early as you can. Ride the trend of their increasing value and see them right before they even hit the ceiling. Do not wait for the price to experience slow increase, or worse, its first decrease—sell them while the stocks are still doing well. This is easier said than done. During such moment, you will feel a strong urge almost like a voice telling you to give it a day more or two days more before selling your stocks, but this same emotional and almost like some form of adrenaline urge is also what can take your profit and investment away.

Penny stocks and price swings

There are two things about price swings or having a high volatility: (1) You can profit a lot; or (2) You can lose everything quickly.

The following list shows which penny stocks usually face huge price swings:

- Companies that deal with inventions and require approval of patent
- Research and development
- Contract basis operations
- Companies engaged in resource explorations
- Those considered as "hot stocks" in the media

The following list shows those that are not subject to dramatic price swings.

- Retail and entertainment companies
- Restaurants
- Mining producers

Many companies can be considered to be between these two lists. Still, regardless of where you invest, the penny stock market as a whole is considered volatile. Factors such as the presence of war or new technology can also greatly influence the price swings of the different penny stocks.

How to Choose the Best Penny Stock Broker

With many stock brokers you can find online, how can you tell the ones that are legitimate and would give you the best deal for your money? There are particular criteria to look for, such as the quality of service, volume and trade restrictions, and the amount of surcharges, among other things.

Transaction fees

This is the cost of trading that you pay to the stock broker. This is usually imposed on every trade that you make. Take note of the real amount of transaction charges. Some may charge a low amount as a promo simply to persuade you to use their service, but then impose a higher rate once the promo period ends.

Surcharges

A small amount of surcharge is usually imposed by brokers on every share at a certain price. Some impose surcharges on shares under a dollar, while others charge it for shares under $2 or $3—this depends on the preference of your stock broker. The amount of surcharge also depends on the broker, so it is important that you choose a broker that has the least overall surcharge. Although the amount of surcharge is usually low, usually just around a cent per share, this can pile up and soon be a big amount. After all, when you invest in penny stocks, you usually have to buy lots of stocks to get a chance of seeing significant gains in profit. For example, if you buy 100,000 shares, with a surcharge of $0.01 per share, you will end up with a total surcharge of $1000.

Volume restrictions

You should be able to trade as many shares as you want without incurring additional charges or, at least only for a small additional fee. After all, when you trade many shares, this automatically means a drastic increase in surcharges.

Trading restrictions

Do not use a brokerage firm that will require you to place your order or trade by phone. Ideally, you should be allowed to invest and trade completely online by using the same trading online platform. This will allow you to take control of everything. Do not worry; most of the legitimate and well-established trading firms will allow you to do this.

Trading frequency rate

There are brokers that charge a small amount per trade; however, they also impose a certain number of trades to be made within a period of time (usually on a per-month basis).

And, if you fail to meet such number, a higher rate will then be imposed.

Minimum deposit requirements

Most online trading platforms require a minimum deposit. Like a bank, some require that the amount of minimum deposit should be maintained at all times. Meaning, you cannot use it even for buying penny stocks. It is simply like a maintaining cost of having an account. Therefore, before you make any deposit, be sure to check the terms and conditions of the contract.

Rating and reviews

Before opening an account with any penny stock broker, take a look at the reviews first. Make a search online and read the rating and reviews given by other investors or traders. Take note that seeing a good rating and positive reviews is also not enough. You should also check the dates when the said reviews were made. If the latest reviews are dated about a year ago, then be cautious and do more research. Investing in penny stocks is already challenging enough; you would not want to deal with other problems simply caused by your stock broker. So stick with well-established trading firms to ensure that you are dealing with a legitimate broker.

Mobile trading

For convenience, it is also good to use a platform that will allow you to trade using your mobile phone. This will allow you to easily access your account and trade anytime, as well as save you the hassle of always going to your computer just to manage your account.

Banking

Knowing the banking terms and conditions is very important when trading online. Some sites accept various ways to deposit money but only have limited options when it comes to withdrawing your funds. PayPal is a popular and trusted method used for transferring money, but not all platforms accept PayPal.

Withdrawal fee

A small withdrawal fee can also be imposed by the broker every time you transfer money to your bank or other third-party service provider (such as PayPal) from your trading account.

Chapter 5: Common Pitfalls and How to Avoid Them

There are mistakes that novice traders or investors in penny stocks always fall for. In fact, even experienced traders still commit some of these errors from time to time. Although such mistakes are part of learning, these mistakes can cost you to lose all your investment.

Here are the common pitfalls to watch out for:

Insufficient research

Many investors gather a few data then quickly make a decision to invest based on such small and limited information. When you do this, it is almost the same as mere guesswork. Chances are you will lose your investment just like the majority who invest in penny stocks.

Just a hobby

Yes, you can deal with penny stocks as a mere hobby. But, most of those who approach penny stocks as a hobby also get a fair result: they lose their money. Success in penny stocks takes a long time of serious study and experience. To expect a wholesome return, you must also dedicate serious effort.

Forcing a trade

Many investors or traders get caught up in the action and make a trade even when the opportunity to make any profit is low. Never force a trade. When you do, you only increase the probability of losing your money.

Inconsistent

Many inexperienced traders are not consistent enough to

follow their plan. By doing so, they end up not knowing whether or not their strategy works, and so they repeat it again. And, usually, they lose again. Such inconsistency usually happens when the price falls. The inexperienced investor fears losing his money, so he suddenly makes changes hoping he could save his investment. The bad thing about this is that such sudden change of decision is usually not backed up with enough research and study, so it tends to make things worse.

Concentrating on good products

Not because a product is good does not mean that it is also the right product for your investment. A good product does not always reflect a company's position or the standing of its stocks in the market. A good product only increases the probability that its company's stocks will also do well in the market. However, like any enterprise, the success of a business means more than having a good product. It also needs marketing efforts, a reliable and strong labor force, excellent employees, a good public image, as well as trusted manufacturers and suppliers, among other things.

Following expert advice

The pieces of advice coming from "experts" should always be taken with a grain of salt. Unfortunately, many of these so-called "experts" oversell their expertise. Therefore, it is no surprise that you can lose a substantial amount of money simply by following expert advice. In fact, the real experts also encounter bad trading days and still commit errors from time to time.

Pump and dump schemes

Pump and dump schemes are rampant in penny stocks. What

they do is they pump the value of a particular stock by making it look like an attractive investment, then once you purchase it, the price drops. They make money out of the sale. Unfortunately, it is you who loses the money and is left with nothing but a low-priced stock with a poor potential of making any profit.

Until now, many traders still fall for a pump and dump scheme, because it is not easy to identify, especially when promoted by one of the "experts." Therefore, to avoid being fooled, you must develop your own understanding and treat everything else that you hear or read as mere suggestions. Also, instead of focusing on the marketing hype, which is the common feature of a pump and dump scheme, focus on facts—focus on the numbers and the company's actual performance.

Short and distort

This is the reverse version of pump and dump. Simply, a person borrows some stocks and sells them. After which, he spreads bad rumors about the said stocks, which will cause its value to drop. Once the price goes down, he then purchases the stocks. This short and distort scheme is rampant in the stock market. And, considering today's age of advanced computer technology, it is easy to do.

Greed

Greed is what misleads even well-experienced traders. After all, why cash out with only 30% profit when you can keep your stocks and earn 200% profit after some time? Well, most the time, after said increase (30%), the price just drops. As a beginner, you should be satisfied with small gains. Focus on having consistent profits regardless whether it is just a small amount and cut down your losses. So long as you have a positive overall result (profits - losses), then you are doing well.

Losing control

It is easy to lose control when you see your investment slowly fading away. But, it is easier to lose control when you encounter a series of positive returns. To be safe, sell some number of your stocks equivalent to at least 30% of your initial investment and then cash out. This can ensure that you can only lose 70% of your initial investment. Another way is to control yourself from buying more and investing more money.

Investing more after a series of losses

Many chase their losses by investing twice or thrice (or even higher) their initial investment to chase their losses, thinking that they can succeed this time. However, the penny stock market does not have a 50-50 probability. It does not have a memory. Just because you lost your first five trades does not mean that your next trade can guarantee any profit. Therefore, every new trade must be backed up with the latest research, study, and analysis of your own.

Investing right after a big increase

Although investing in penny stocks whose value has just recently increased significantly can bring some nice income, this is not effective in the long run, especially when you have no other basis but the mere fact of its recent increase in value.

Investing after a significant decrease in price

Some investors understand volatility as something that is balanced: When the price decreases, it will soon increase. Therefore, some traders invest immediately right after a significant decrease in the price of a particular stock, hoping that it will increase in the near future. However, volatility does not work this way, and the high volatility of penny stocks is never balanced. There are stock prices that fall down and never get any chance to go up again. Then the company declares bankruptcy, closes down, and you lose everything.

Averaging down

Averaging down is when you buy a certain stock, and when its value decreases, you buy more stocks at a lower price. The good thing about this is that your price per share (on average) is guaranteed to be lower; however, the fact remains that you have invested money on something whose price has just decreased and that you have not earned any income even by buying for the second time, and there is no assurance that the price will now pick up. In fact, things usually get complicated because even after the first decrease in price, it is followed by another drop, then another. By chasing down the price and spending more, there is a good chance that you will just lose your investment. Therefore, avoid averaging down. Research as much as you can about the stocks and the company concerned before you purchase any stock. This will increase your probability of choosing the right stocks to invest in without having to chase down the price of a particular stock.

Depending on penny stock newsletters

Do not make any investment decision based on newsletters that you receive from so-called "experts" or "trusted" websites. Such newsletters are usually part of a pump and dump fraud. The company pays people to promote their stocks through newsletters in order to draw interest to its stocks. Once the price of its stocks increases due to the interest that the newsletter is able to draw, it sells its shares at a premium price, then the price falls down after the sale. The effect: They earn a nice profit, and you get to hold a losing stock.

Sticking to known strategies

Why do you think people continue to develop systems on how to make money on penny stocks despite the so many suggested tips and strategies that you can find online? The reason is simple: Because until now, there is still no established and sure strategy that can guarantee one to make a huge amount of profit by investing in penny stocks. So, learn the different tips and suggestions, and then develop your own strategy.

Conclusion

Thank for making it through to the end of this book, let's hope it was informative and able to provide you with all of the tools you need to achieve your goals whatever they may be.

The next step is to apply everything that you know about penny stocks. So, it is time for you to open an account with a trusted and reliable platform, invest some money, begin trading, and start making money!

Finally, if you found this book useful in any way, a review on Amazon is always appreciated!

Description

Learn the basics and avoid the common pitfalls that have caused many investors to lose their money. *Penny Stocks* is your one-stop guide to everything that you need to know about investing in and trading penny stocks. It is a handy manual for both new and experienced investors. It will teach you how to identify the best penny stocks to invest in, the different factors that affect volatility, how to minimize your losses and make more money, as well as many other things.

www.ingramcontent.com/pod-product-compliance
Lightning Source LLC
Chambersburg PA
CBHW061230180526
45170CB00003B/1232